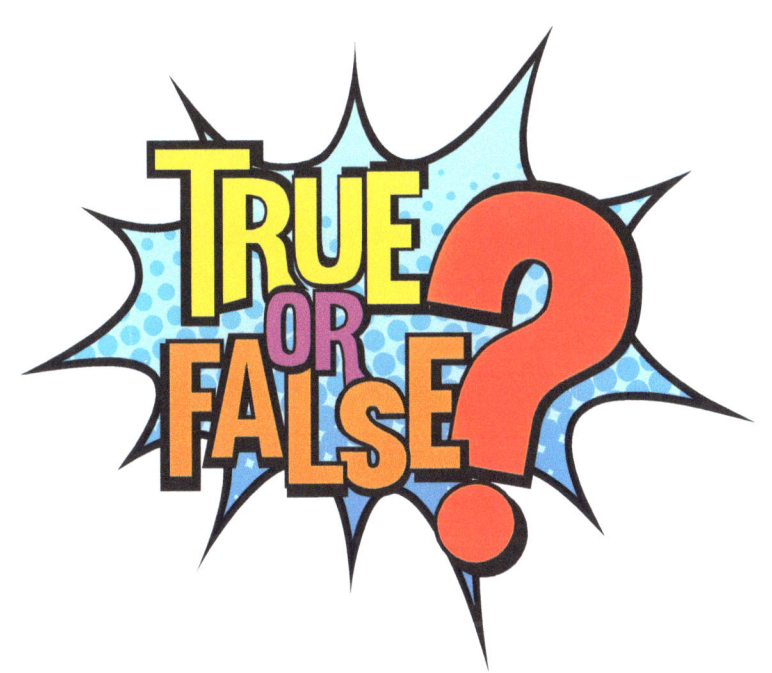

Co-published by agreement between Shi Tu Hui and World Book, Inc.

Shi Tu Hui
Room 1807, Block 1,
#3 West Dawang Road
Chaoyang District, Beijing 100025
P.R. China

World Book, Inc.
180 North LaSalle Street
Suite 900
Chicago, Illinois 60601
USA

Copyright © 2024. All rights reserved. This volume may not be reproduced in whole or in part in any form without prior written permission from the publishers.

WORLD BOOK and the GLOBE DEVICE are registered trademarks or trademarks of World Book, Inc.

Library of Congress Cataloging-in-Publication Data for this volume has been applied for.

True or False? (set #4)
ISBN: 978-0-7166-5417-9 (set, hc.)

Ancient Egypt
ISBN: 978-0-7166-5418-6 (hc.)

Also available as:
ISBN: 978-0-7166-5428-5 (e-book)
ISBN: 978-0-7166-5438-4 (soft cover)

Staff

Executive Committee

President
Geoff Broderick

Vice President, Editorial
Tom Evans

Vice President, Finance
Molly Stedron

Vice President, International and Marketing
Eddy Kisman

Vice President, Technology and Operations
Jason Dole

Director, Human Resources
Bev Ecker

Editorial

Writer
Lauren Kelliher

Manager, New Content
Jeff De La Rosa

Associate Manager, New Content
William D. Adams

Curriculum Designer
Caroline Davidson

Proofreader
Nathalie Strassheim

Graphics and Design

Coordinator, Design Development & Production:
Brenda Tropinski

Senior Visual Communications Designer
Melanie Bender

Senior Media Editor
Rosalia Bledsoe

True or False?

The Egyptian pyramids are the oldest and largest stone buildings in the world.

The earliest surviving pyramid, called the Step Pyramid, was built about 2650 B.C. The largest is the Great Pyramid at Giza, reaching 450 feet (140 meters) high and covering 13 acres (5 hectares) at the base.

True or False?

Ancient Egyptian temples were built to be huge gathering places for people to worship.

FALSE!

Temples were considered the homes of the *deities* (gods and goddesses) or dead kings. Priests in ancient Egypt did not hold services for the public; they served the deity or king. Most Egyptians worshiped at home.

Frequent flooding along the mighty Nile River made farming difficult.

FALSE!

The Nile's annual floods deposited a 6-mile- (10-kilometer-) wide strip of fertile black soil on each riverbank. The soil was perfect for farming and led the ancient Egyptians to call their country Kemet, meaning Black Land, after the dark soil.

True or False?

The first Egyptian capital was called Memphis.

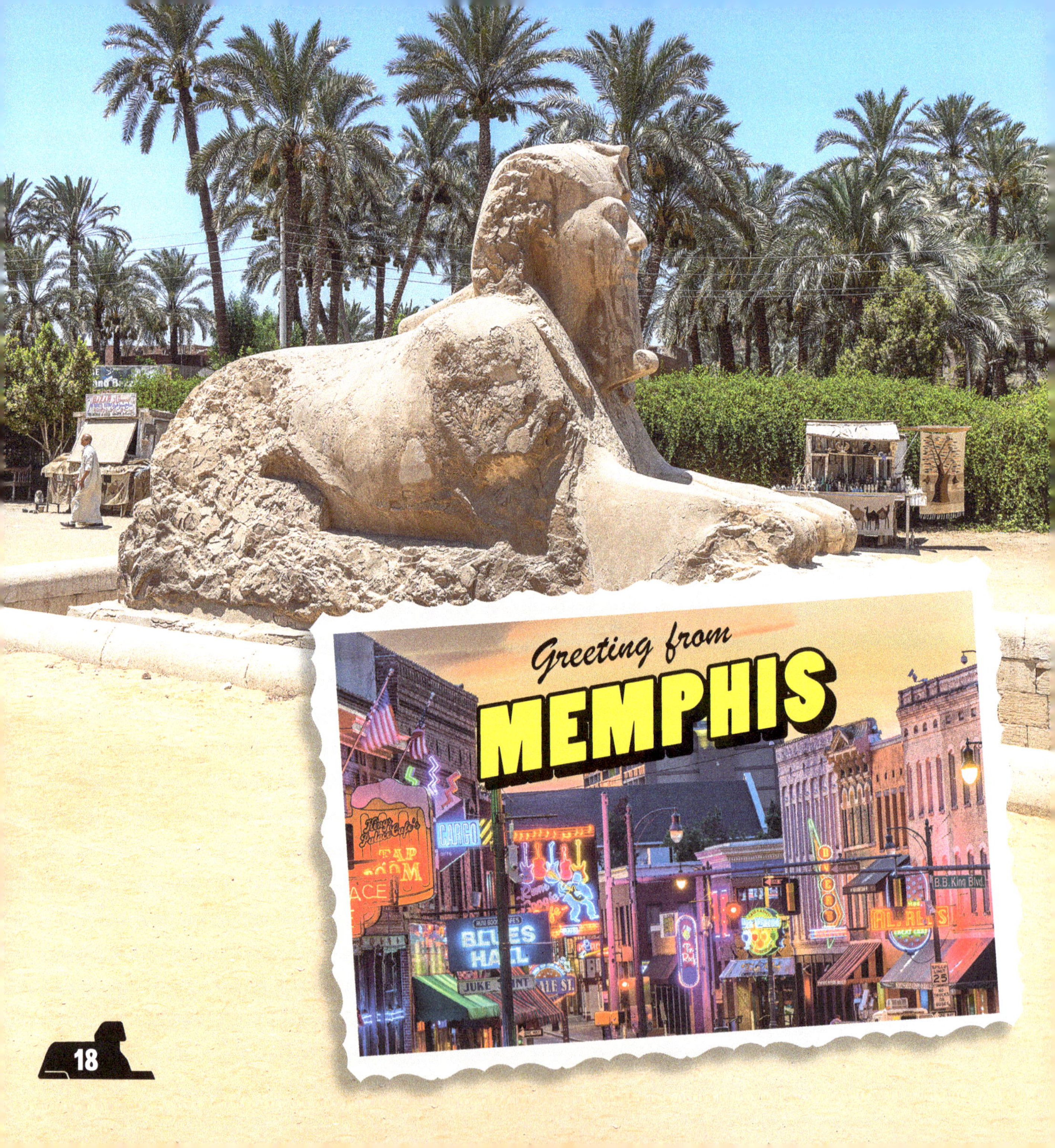
Greeting from
MEMPHIS
CARGO
BLUES HALL
B.B. King Blvd

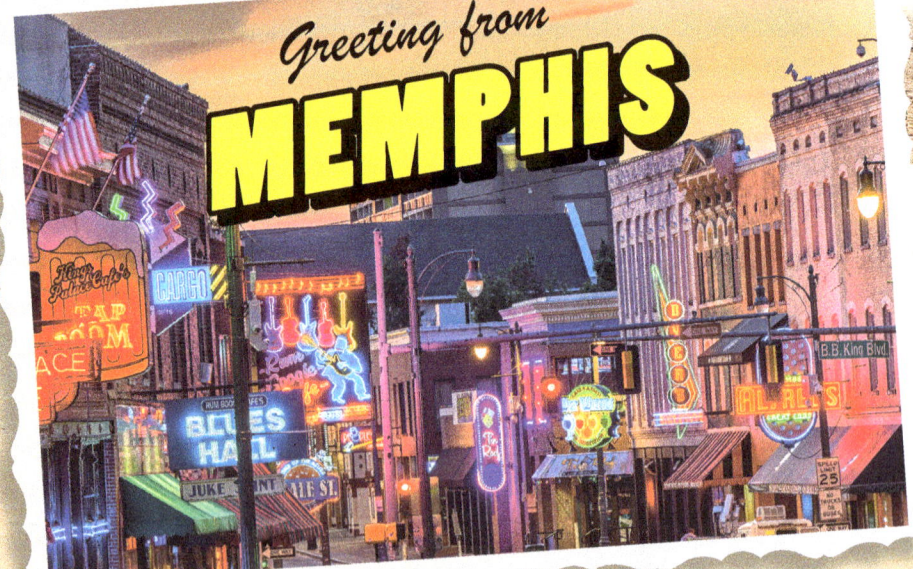

The legendary Home of the Blues wasn't the first Memphis! The original Memphis was founded around 3000 B.C. as the first capital of ancient Egypt. Memphis, Tennessee, was named for the ancient city.

The ancient Egyptians communicated using an early form of emojis.

Well, sort of. Today, we use picture symbols called emojis to express ideas or emotions. Ancient Egyptians wrote in *hieroglyphics*, picture symbols that stand for specific ideas and sounds. Hieroglyphics form a language system much more complex than emojis, which have no set meanings.

True or False?

The last ruler of ancient Egypt was a woman.

TRUE!

Cleopatra VII served as the last ruler of the Ptolemaic *dynasty* (ruling family). Cleopatra was intelligent, charming, witty, and ambitious. As pharaoh, she regained Egyptian territory from the Romans during her marriage to the Roman leader Marc Antony.

Ancient Egyptian women had many of the same rights as men.

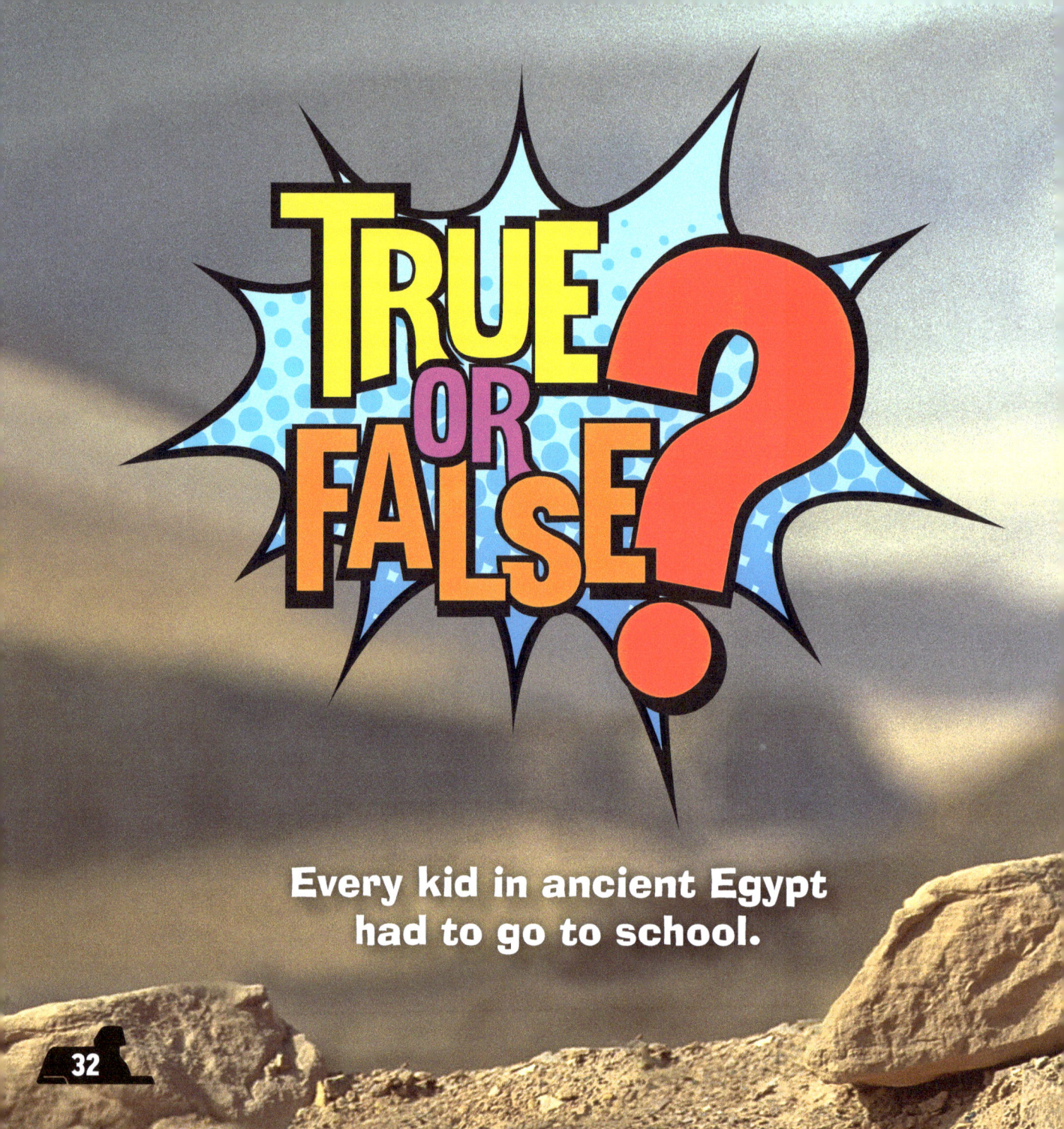

True or False?

Every kid in ancient Egypt had to go to school.

FALSE!

Few children went to school besides those of wealthy families. Those who went to school became scribes for the government, temples, or even the palace. Other boys learned *trades* (skilled work) from their fathers or master craftsmen. Many girls learned household skills.

The famed Alexandrian Library was the greatest collection of scrolls in the ancient world.

The Alexandrian Library held about 500,000 papyrus scrolls on astrology, geography, and many other subjects. Papyrus is the world's first paperlike material, invented by the ancient Egyptians. The magnificent library and accompanying museum helped make the city one of the greatest cultural centers of ancient times.

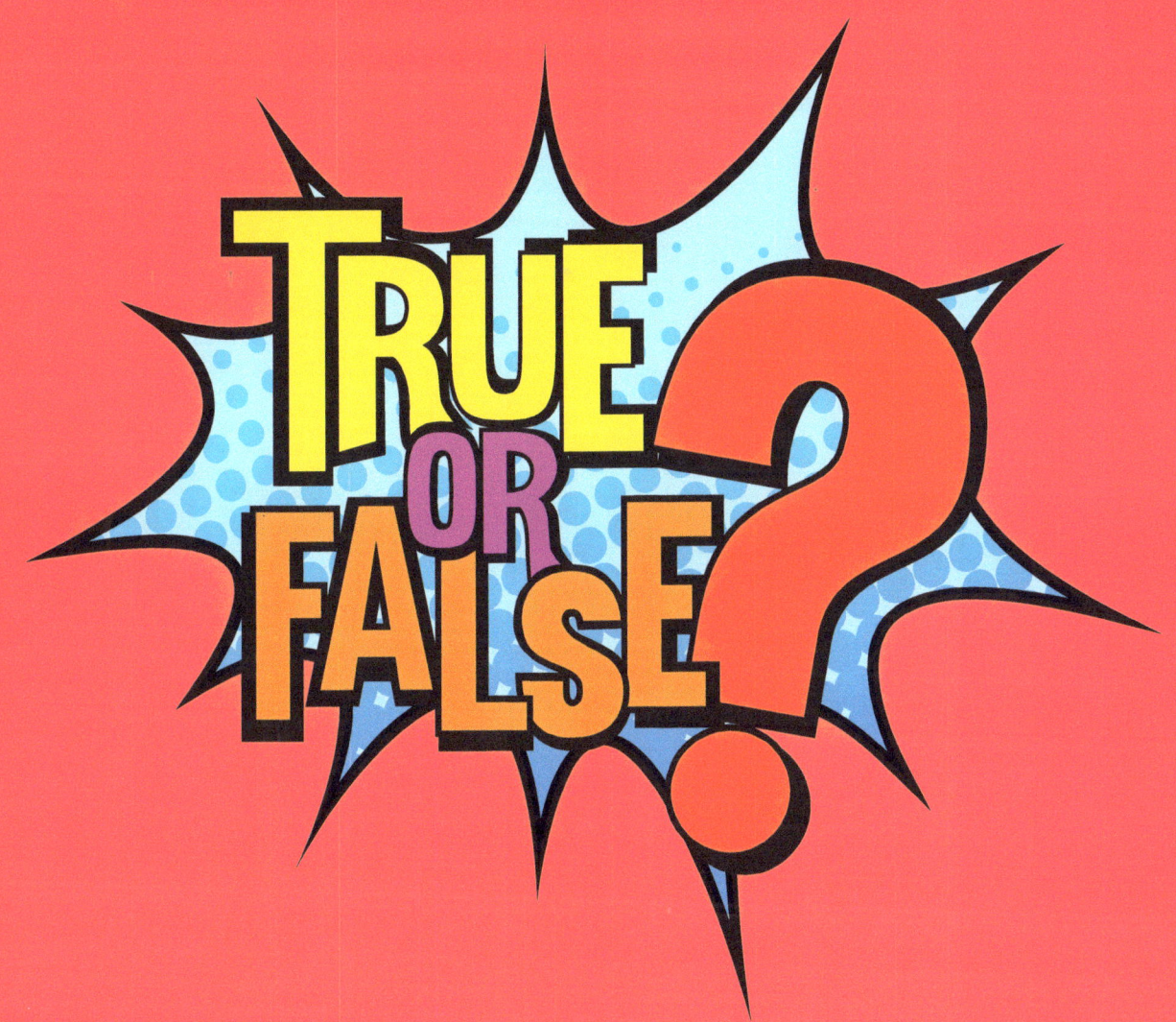

Ancient Egyptian doctors created the first *vaccines* (injections to prevent illness).

The first vaccine was created by the British physician Edward Jenner in 1796, to prevent the disease smallpox. But, ancient Egyptian doctors were the first physicians to study the human body scientifically. They studied human anatomy and could set broken bones, care for wounds, and treat illnesses.

TRUE OR FALSE?

Ancient Egyptians loved eyeliner.

Both men and women of ancient Egypt used a variety of cosmetics. They outlined their eyes with gray, black, or green paint. Many rocked a red lip color, hair dye, and nail polish, too. Don't forget the jewelry! Bracelets, necklaces, and rings were worn to adorn.

TRUE OR FALSE?

Mummies are a fake idea made up for horror movies.

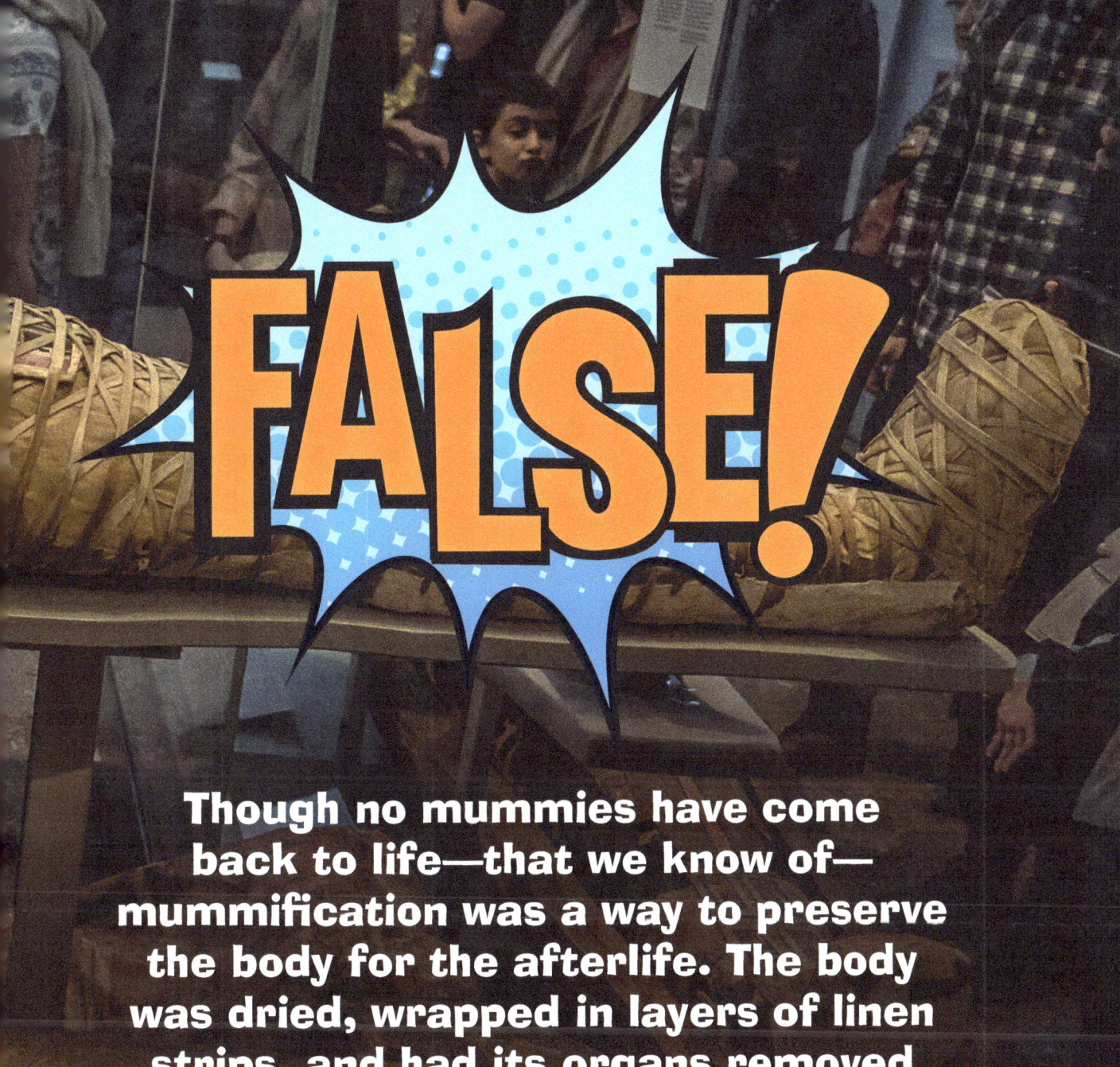

FALSE!

Though no mummies have come back to life—that we know of—mummification was a way to preserve the body for the afterlife. The body was dried, wrapped in layers of linen strips, and had its organs removed before being placed in a coffin.

True or False?

The afterlife was of little importance to ancient Egyptians.

Quite the opposite!
Ancient Egyptians believed in life after death, which led to much preparation for death and burial. They invested great effort in the construction of the pyramids and other great tombs.

The gods and goddesses of ancient Egypt were pictured as part animal and part human.

Many *deities* (divine beings) were pictured with the heads or heads and bodies of animals. The choice of animal suggested a quality the god or goddess also possessed. For example, the god of mummification, Anubis, had the head of a jackal, an animal associated with death.

TRUE OR FALSE?

The mystical Book of the Dead was a spell book.

The Book of the Dead contained prayers, hymns, and spells. The collections of texts included information to guide souls through the afterlife, protect them from evil, and provide for their needs. Passages from the book were written or carved on walls of tombs.

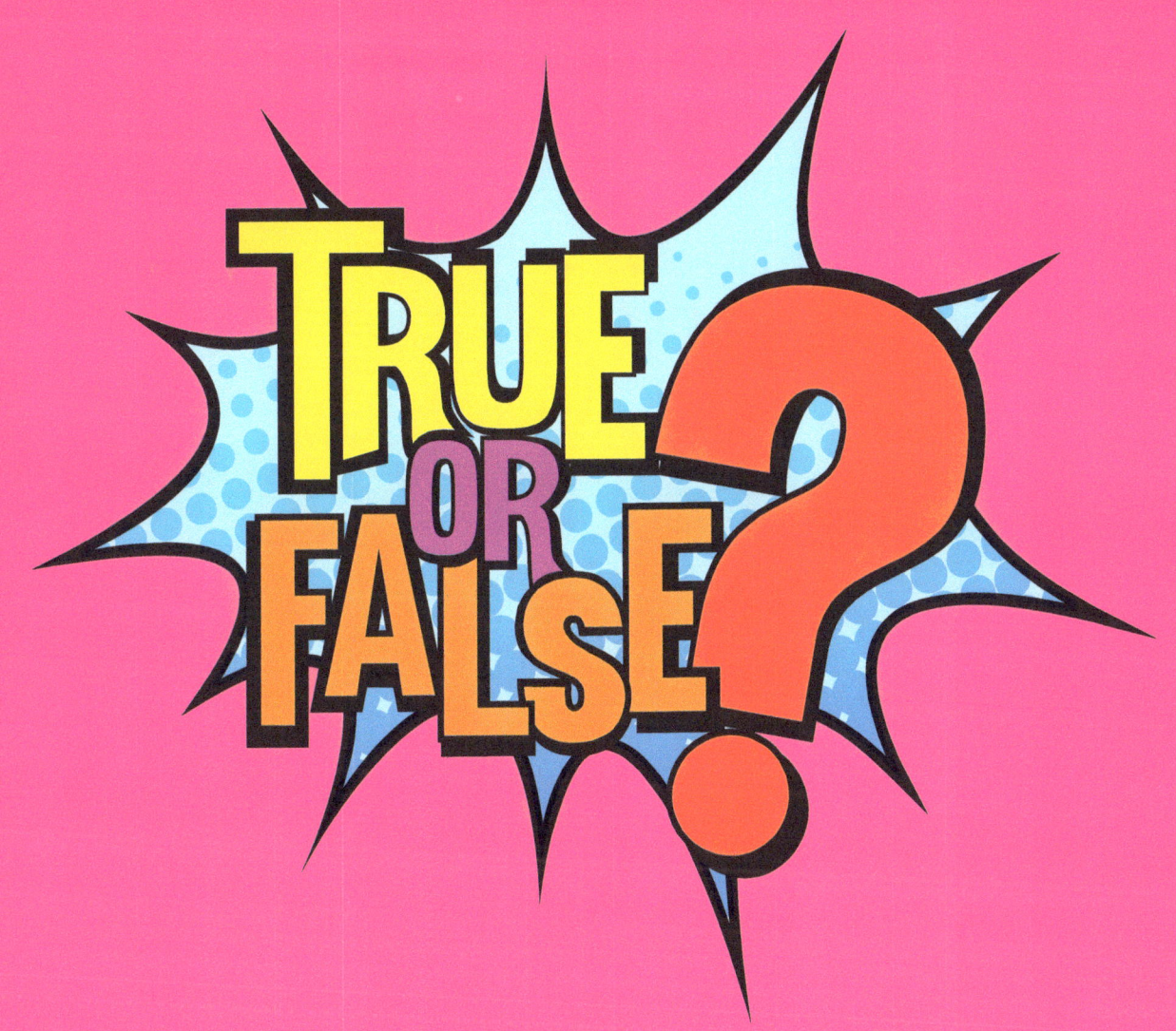

Egypt became an *agricultural* (farming) power due to its plentiful rainfall.

Very little rain fell in ancient Egypt, bordered by deserts and the Mediterranean Sea. But farmers didn't let that stop them from growing crops most of the year. They irrigated land by building canals that brought fresh water from the Nile to the fields.

To travel on the Nile, Egyptians crafted boats out of reeds and pushed them along the river with poles.

TRUE!

Ancient Egyptian boats made many advancements as time went on. Egyptians later used oars to move their boats. Around 3200 B.C., they invented sails to harness the wind. They began building their ships from wood a few hundred years later.

True or False?

Complicated hieroglyphics were the only way ancient Egyptians wrote things down, even in their diaries!

FALSE!

Though there were thousands of picture symbols in Egyptian hieroglyphics, they were mainly used to record official texts or *inscribe* (write on) monuments and temples. Everyday writing made use of simpler hieroglyphic forms called hieratic and demotic.

True or False?

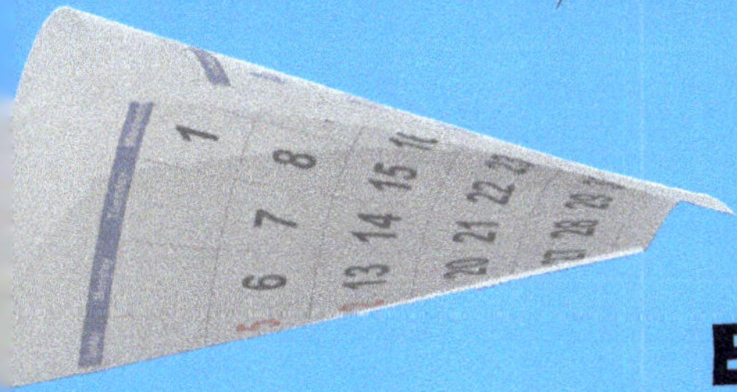

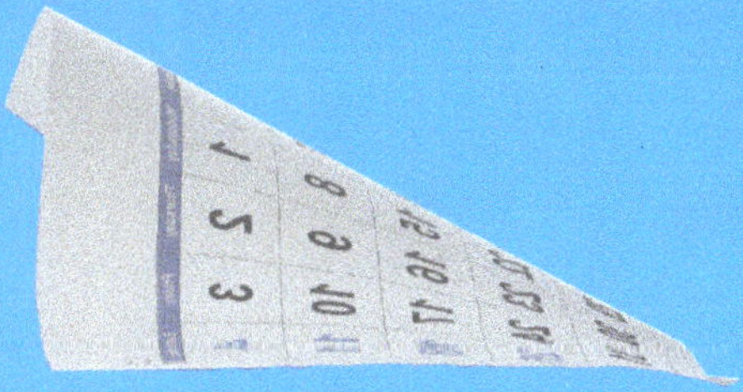

Egyptians had a 365-day calendar based on a flood and a star.

The Nile started its annual flooding after the star we call Sirius appeared on the eastern horizon—on June 20th each year. Ancient Egyptians pretty much invented the 365-day calendar we use today.

TRUE OR FALSE?

Queen Hatshepsut emphasized her power by portraying herself as a goddess in public art.

Because Egyptians believed their kings were divine, Hatshepsut justified her role as pharaoh by claiming to be the god Amun's daughter. To emphasize her authority as pharaoh, however, she had herself *depicted* (shown) as a man on monuments—complete with a beard!

For a long time, people forgot how to read hieroglyphics.

After Egypt came under Roman rule in 30 B.C., the ability to read hieroglyphics was quickly lost. In 1799, a rock called the Rosetta Stone was found with the same message written in three languages: hieroglyphics, demotic, and Greek. By 1822, a French scholar named Jean-François Champollion had studied the stone to decipher hieroglyphics.

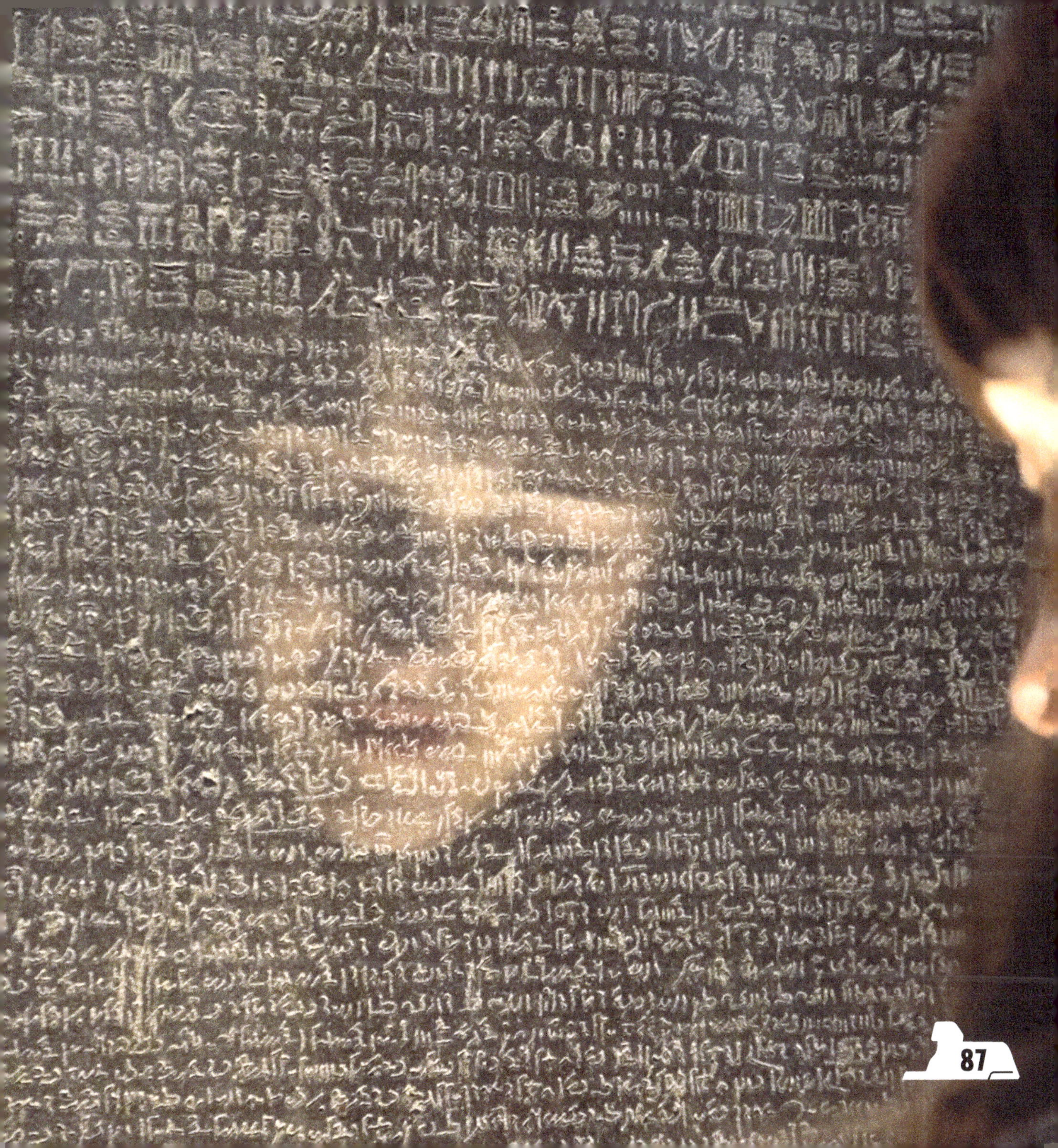

The ancient Egyptians revered and worshiped cats.

Some did! The goddess Bastet was pictured as a woman with the head of a cat. Carefully mummified cats have been found at many Egyptian sites.

DID YOU KNOW...

Ancient Egyptians jotted notes on broken pieces of pottery called ostraca.

Hundreds of thousands of workers built **the Great Pyramid** layer by layer, hauling 2 million limestone blocks weighing an average of 2 ½ tons (2.3 metric tons) each.

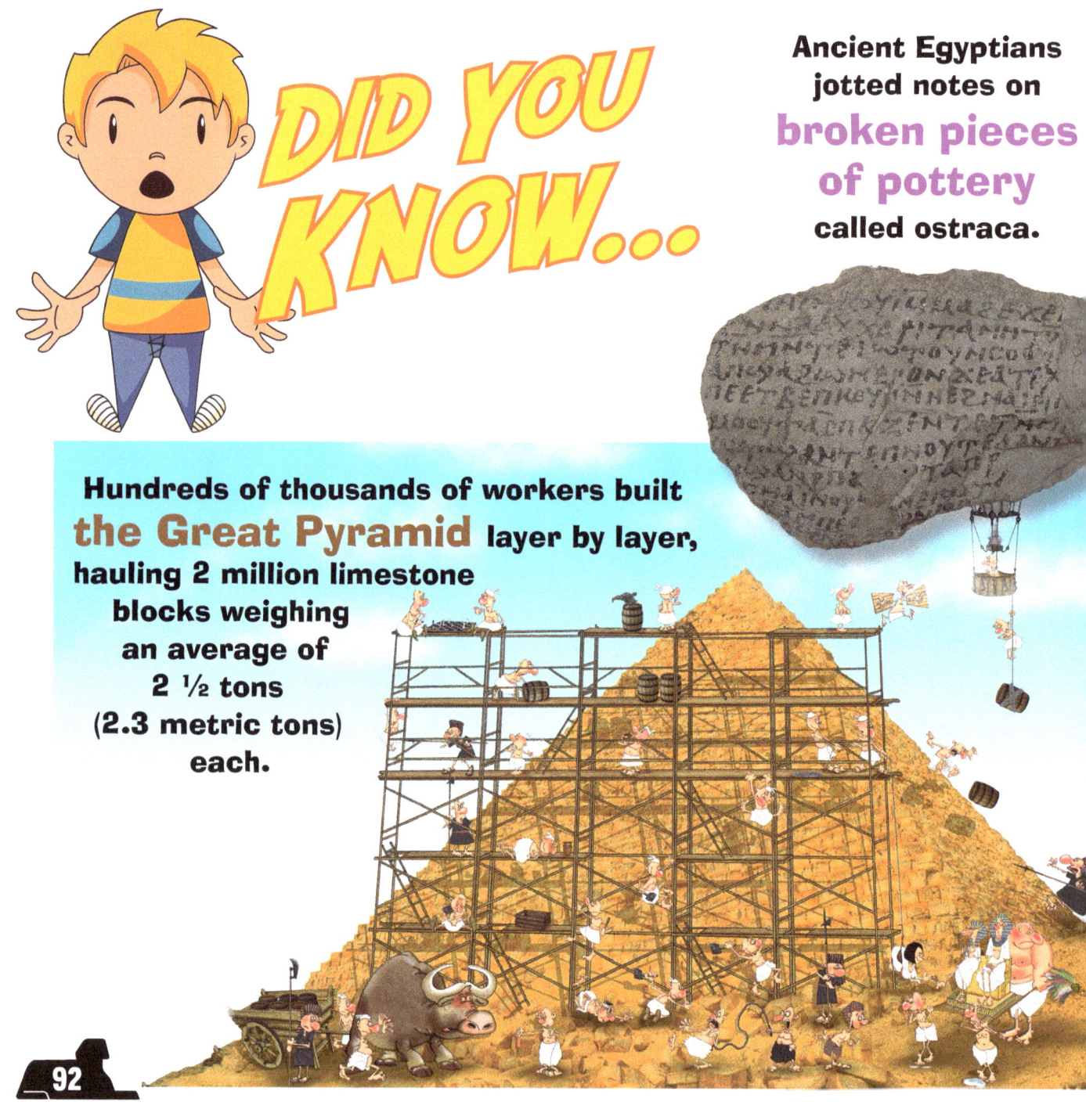

Ancient Egyptians played **a game called senet** that was very similar to today's backgammon.

On hot nights, **Egyptians slept on the roofs** of their houses, where it was cooler.

The Alexandrian Library was destroyed in a war. Not a trace of it remains today!

ENGAGE YOUR READER

GUIDED READING PROMPTS

Before Reading
- Allow readers to scan the text and discuss what they notice so far. Highlight the structure of this text and explain that the answers include both evidence and reasoning that support the claim of true or false.
- Explain the literacy skill: *Sometimes authors write a claim and then use evidence and reasoning to help make their point clear. Look for these elements as you read!*

During Reading
- Read each statement and provide time to discuss whether readers believe it to be true or false before turning the page to learn the facts.
- As you read, model how to identify the claims, evidence, and reasoning in the text. Prompt your readers to identify these features as they explore the text, too.
- Encourage readers to further discuss their learning by pausing to discuss surprising information.

After Reading
- Prompt your readers to connect, extend, and challenge their thinking about the text:
    - What will you take away from reading this text?
    - What changes in your thinking happened while reading and learning?
    - What is still challenging your thinking? What questions or wonderings do you still have?

LOOK BACK!
- Prompt readers to look back through the text to identify examples of interesting or thought-provoking claims.
- Challenge readers to explain what makes these examples so engaging.

CURRICULUM CONNECTIONS
These questions and tasks support the following English/Language Arts skills:
- Determining what a text says both explicitly and implicitly
- Citing specific evidence when drawing conclusions
- Interpreting words and phrases used in a text
- Analyzing how the structure of a text affects how it is read.

LITERACY SKILL

Authors make their claims stronger by supporting them with evidence and reasoning.
- A claim is a statement of truth.
- Evidence includes the facts or information that prove whether the claim is true.
- Reasoning includes any logical explanation that describes how the evidence supports the claim.

Example from the text: Pages 36-39
- Claim: The Alexandrian Library of contained the greatest collection of scrolls in the ancient world.
- Evidence: The library held about 500,000 papyrus scrolls and accompanied a museum.
- Reasoning: Information ranged from astrology to geography and many other subjects, making the library one of the greatest collections at the time.

EXTEND THROUGH WRITING

Challenge readers to create their own True/False questions and answers about ancient Egypt.
- Have readers use a trusted reference, such as www.worldbookonline.com, to research information related to ancient Egypt. Encourage readers to look for key details, fun facts, or surprising features that would make strong True or False statements.
- Give readers one notecard for each claim they research.
- Direct readers to write the claim on the front of the notecard. On the back, readers should describe why that claim is true or false using evidence and reasoning from their research.

MORE WAYS TO ENGAGE!

- Play a game! After considering each claim, have readers signify "true" with a thumb up and "false" with a thumb down. Keep score to see who knows their facts about ancient Egypt the best!
  - Develop collaboration skills by grouping readers together into teams.
- Further discuss any True/False claims that revealed readers' misconceptions. Focus the conversation on *why* they initially thought what they did and how the text helped them learn.

Acknowledgments

Cover	© Art Form/Shutterstock; © Stock Smart Start/Shutterstock; © Roquillo Tebar, Shutterstock
4-9	© Shutterstock
10-11	© Justinas/Adobe Stock
12-31	© Shutterstock
32-33	© Bill Freeman, Alamy Images
34-35	© efesenko/Adobe Stock; © World History Archive/Alamy Images
36-37	© SP Collection/Alamy Images
38-39	© Shaiith/Shutterstock; © North Wind Picture Archives/Alamy Images
40-41	© Shutterstock
42-43	© De Agostini Picture Library/agefotostock
44-45	© agefotostock/Alamy Images
46-47	Metropolitan Museum of Art
48-55	© Shutterstock
56-57	© The Print Collector/Alamy Images
58-59	Metropolitan Museum of Art
60-61	© Alain Guilleux, Alamy Images
62-63	© Paul Williams, funkyfood London/Alamy Images
64-65	Metropolitan Museum of Art
66-67	© Middle East/Alamy Images
68-69	© Paul Williams, funkyfood London/Alamy Images
70-71	© Images & Stories/Alamy Images
72-73	© Album/Alamy Images
74-75	© Fedor Selivanov, Shutterstock; © Lakeview Images/Alamy Images
76-77	© nagelestock.com/Alamy Images; © kostasgr/Shutterstock; © vovan/Shutterstock
78-79	© Art Directors & TRIP/Alamy Images; © kostasgr/Shutterstock
80-81	© Chronicle/Alamy Images
82-87	© Shutterstock
88-89	© SuperStock/Alamy Images
90-91	© Vladimir Zadvinskii, Shutterstock
92-93	Metropolitan Museum of Art; © Glukoejik/Shutterstock; © design_mst/Shutterstock; © Iconic Bestiary/Shutterstock; © German Vizulis, Shutterstock
94	© ShiipArt/Shutterstock; © NeMaria/Shutterstock

www.ingramcontent.com/pod-product-compliance
Lightning Source LLC
Chambersburg PA
CBHW061407090426
42740CB00023B/3471